OXFORD
UNIVERSITY PRESS

Unusual Buildings

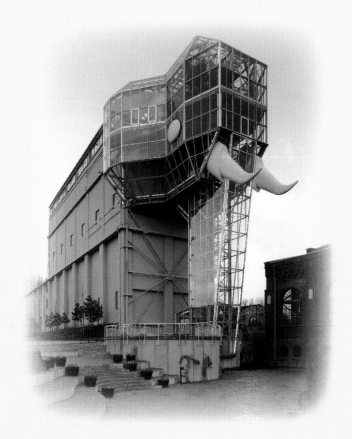

Anne-Marie Parker

Contents

Introduction 3
Pyramids 4
Igloos 6
Adobe Houses 8
Boswell Bottle House 10
Junk Castle 12
Leaning Tower of Pisa 14
The Glass Elephant 16
A Tent That Isn't a Tent 18
Futuristic Buildings 20
Index 24

Introduction

There are many buildings in the world that you might think unusual. You might think this because they are not the shape you are used to. Or you might think they are not made from materials you are used to.

Have a look at the buildings in this book. They are many different shapes. Some are made from snow, mud, glass bottles or even junk.

Pyramids

A long time ago in Ancient Egypt, people built buildings called pyramids. Pyramids were built of stone.

The people of Ancient Egypt buried their kings inside pyramids.

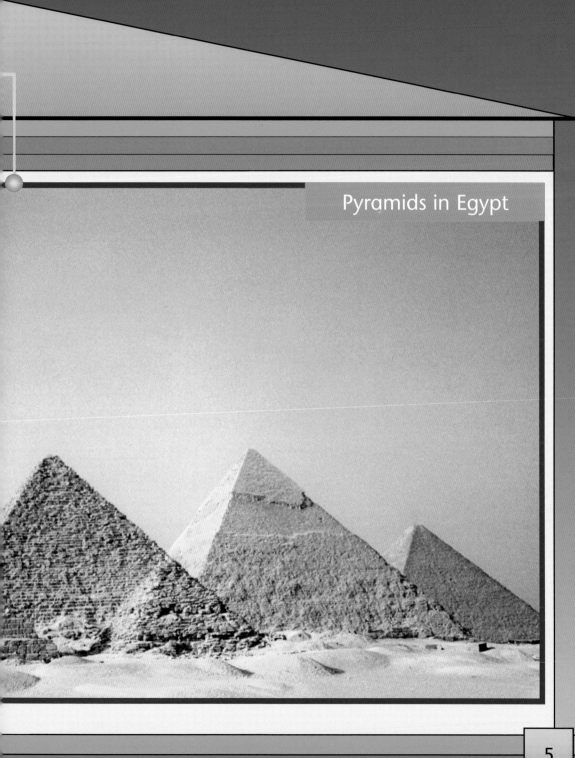

Pyramids in Egypt

Igloos

An igloo lit up at night

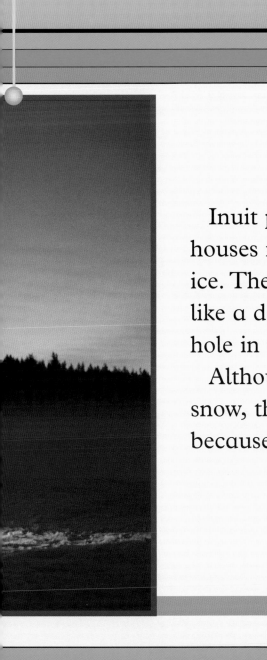

Inuit people sometimes build houses made from snow and ice. These buildings are shaped like a dome. There is a small hole in the top to let fresh air in. Although igloos are made of snow, they are warm inside because of their shape.

Adobe Houses

Adobe is a kind of clay used to make bricks. A long time ago, people in Mexico built houses made of these bricks. They mixed the clay with straw and grass to make the bricks strong. Then they left the bricks in the sun to dry.

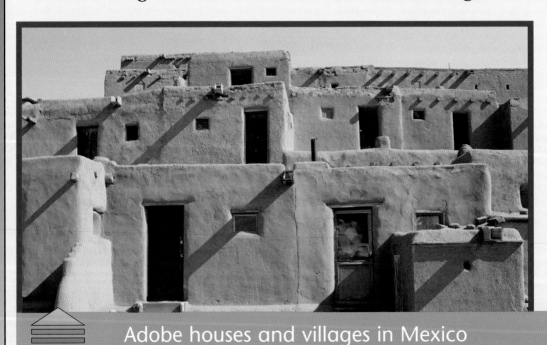

Adobe houses and villages in Mexico

Adobe houses are found in countries that do not have a lot of rain. Too much rain would wash the clay houses away.

Boswell Bottle House

All the walls in the Boswell Bottle House are made of old bottles stuck together.

During the day, light shines into the house through the glass bottles. At night, the air trapped in the bottles keeps the house warm.

Boswell Bottle House in the UK is
made of 500,000 glass bottles.

Junk Castle

Junk Castle, USA

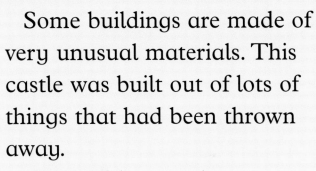

Some buildings are made of very unusual materials. This castle was built out of lots of things that had been thrown away.

The builders used tree branches and old sheets of tin. They used scraps of metal from old tractors and wheelbarrows, and even an old washing machine. This is called junk.

Leaning Tower of Pisa

A long time ago, the Roman people built a bell tower. This tower was built in a small town called Pisa in Italy. Over the years the tower slowly began to lean. Every year the building leans over a little bit more.

This tower is known as
the Leaning Tower of Pisa.

The Glass Elephant is a building in Germany. It was built to look like an elephant. The builders used lots of glass to build the body and head.

The Glass Elephant building even has eyes and tusks.

A Tent That Isn't a Tent

You might think that this building looks like a tent. It does have a 'skin' like a tent, but it is also made out of lots of steel. It cannot be moved easily like a tent can. The steel makes this building strong so that it will not blow over in a storm.

Scientists work inside this building.

Futuristic Buildings

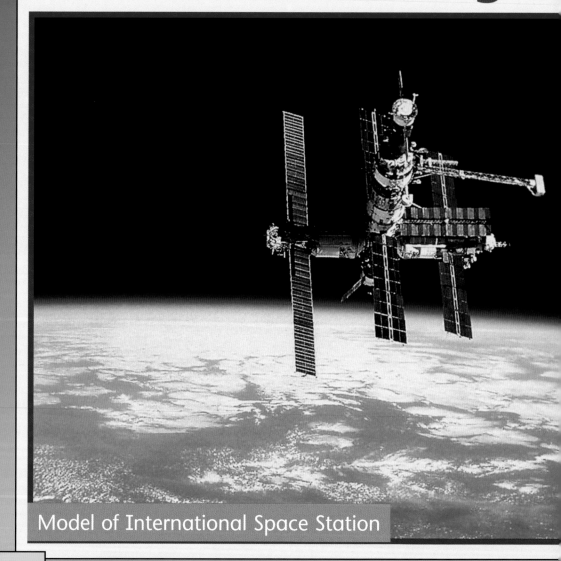

Model of International Space Station

We do not know what buildings will look like in the future. Perhaps they will be made so that we can live under the sea, or in space. We might live in something like this space station.

Can you imagine living on the moon or on one of the other planets in space? What would the buildings look like and what would they be made of? Would they look unusual?

What do you think?

Index

air 7, 10

clay 8, 9

countries 9

dome 7

Egypt 4, 5

Germany 16

ice 7

Inuit 7

Italy 14

kings 4

light 10

materials 3, 13

Mexico 8

moon 22

Pisa 14, 15

scientists 18, 19

snow 3, 7

space 20-22

sun 8